As They Say

As They Say

ROBERT MANERY

BLAZEVOX[BOOKS]
Buffalo, New York

Interior design and typesetting by Geoffrey Gatza
Cover Art: Robyn Laba

First Edition
ISBN: 978-1-60964-459-8
Library of Congress Control Number: 2023950083

BlazeVOX [books]
131 Euclid Ave
Kenmore, NY 14217
Editor@blazevox.org

publisher of weird little books

BlazeVOX [books]

blazevox.org

21 20 19 18 17 16 15 14 13 12 01 02 03 04 05 06 07 08 09 10 11

BlazeVOX

for Isaac & Robyn

CONTENTS

As They Say

Equivocation

i

swear
in and in
and in

upon
which place
there must be

three companions
of whom
all have I
earned

without all
or any
one of
them

we ought
always to
see that
nothing

is the chief
question
and
bitterly inveigh

in all
in the world
we begin

ii

an enunciative
speech
teaches

either
conceived
in the mind

or uttered
by words
we may say

as when
I think
with myself
these words

as when
I utter
these words
with my mouth

as if
I should set
the same down
in writing

when we
mingle
together
knowing

nevertheless
I know not

understanding
within myself
these other words

iii

all in word
or all in writing

the mind
remains the same

not altered
at all

to speak
lose suddenly

my speech
before spoken

impossibility
or other respects

the party
to whom I speak

understands not
knowing all to be true

any fault
we affirm

there is no lie
other than before

but when asked
of none

without a lie
speak

and by his speech
understand

than that which
others understand

although
discourteously uttered

iv

except
we understand

not everything
asked is granted

not expressed
but understood

thrust these words
some ordinary

equivocations when
we use such words

according to
the accustomed

manner may
have two

senses besides
the words uttered

cannot be
understood

do not excuse
a lie too

severe
and scrupulous

allow some
reservation

or illation
which they call

desirous of
some secret words

or was at that time
irresolute

both opinions
are possible

by their gravity
maturity, judgement

indifferency, incorruption
the impugners

carping at
just equivocations

v

ways whereby
without a lie

a truth may
be covered

although the
hearer

conceive the
other

which is
false

the like
unto this

if one should
be asked

yield one
and conceal

the other

Dilemmas

i

adversity
inevitably
obliges

not sincere
but actual
dependence

counters
feigned
reluctance

subsiding
subsiding

ii

so rashly
countered

but so
adversely
precise

this premise
conceivably
adverse

or
foreseen

iii

reluctant
disasters

imply
avowedly

familiar
foresight

rigorously
thin

iv

each exposed
consolation

without knowledge
without aversion

seems exact
indeed

never uttering
never diminishing

else
elusive

indeed
seemed

yet we
grasp

and we
grasp

within

v

uttered indeed
or obversely
measured

certain
or rather
ascertain

assuage
or rather
assume

an elusive
imagining
minded

between but
if an apparent
between

an apparent
and another
implies another

or else settled
utterly settled

vi

diminished difference
involves difference
measured without
consideration

never exact
never without
merely uttering
merely different

never settled
nor considered
else forgiven

vii

implicit friction
persuades counterparts
nor attempts pleasure
but abeyance attempted

deliberated
yet disliking
such subtle worry
suggestively missing

such reliance
grips unpalatable worry
and worry grips this
mooted clamour

viii

paused abeyance
harnesses mooted
deliberation plausibly

either deliberate
or arbitrary
worry

a moment's
resilience riddles
consequences

either subtle
or fictive
moments

answer
estimable
consequences

enjoying
disliking
abeyance

assumed clamour
quiets attempted
worry

unpalatable
yet palpable
as riddles

missing riddles
grasps
either answer

Let's Sit Down and Lie to One Another

The witness shuffled,
pretended to misunderstand
the questions. Bailey replied
that he had heard so.

I begin to doubt
you won't tell a downright
fib for the world; no
Jesuit ever went beyond

you, in manners as well
as in words; but answer
faithfully to every question.
He said he hadn't?

After quibbling, shuffling,
and procrastinating,
the ploughman who ploughs
crooked was said

to prevaricate. The Court
found him such a false
rascal. 'I see', exclaimed the
Judge, 'but, I shall trounce

you before we part'.
'What did you see?
A car you recognize?'
I made a noise.

Make up your mind
what you will ask him,
for ghosts will stand
no shilly-shallying.

Their deformity appeared
through the finest colors.
I'm lost if you don't
dissemble a little.

Any wowser who wears
a black coat and a plug
hat. Some pander, perjure,
cozen, quack, or rob.

'Let's sit down and lie
to one another'. There was
no established procedure.
All you needed was fear,

I answered evasively.

As They Say
for Peter Culley

Except by those
    who go out
with the hounds,
    the land is thin
of timber.
    Without salt
(as they say).
    I've got to find
a stick of stovewood
    or a piece of iron;
somewhere there be roses
    and roses. Now neek
rows briskly
    out the lums
consisting of gum, oak,
    Banksia, and thorn,
of iron for scarfs, garters, gold.
    He complains
and I plain not.
    Out with it,
Mr. Farrell.
    When naked
of all but his shirt
    or eating gold,
as the old saying is.
    Naturally I'm off
my nut, especially
    as I do all
these things by myself,
    wandering along the foggy
Embarcadero. I know

that I am somewhere
in the fifties, and that I
was born
on a Monday.
A chain of proofs
must have their
commencement somewhere.
It was most
absurd of you
to offer it!
Some gigantic kind
of natural alchemical
laboratory during the time,
times, and half a time
then its complete
reversal was also true.
The Rima is not yet
well known to the
botanists. Hence
the endless repetitions.
Long curved narrow valleys
are especially troublesome.
O, rocks! she said.
Tell us in plain words.
The eggs of small birds
being liable to cool
more quickly. The question
was inextricably twisted up
with the other question.
That lets me into a little
fact about you!

She came in
    like a swan
swimming its way.
    I am not in
the clouds, dear;
    I am only anxious.
This year several
    have been familiar
about the house, penning
    the contours, and outlines
with a more even and
    acute touch.
Brushwood of myrtle,
    heath, and arbutus,
traps woven
    out of reeds
and buttressed
    sharp fits
of the stone,
    with our hill-side retreat.
In the distance
    a flock of black-faced
ibises are feeding.
    There is considerable
doubt at this writing
    that my hog
has been bred,
    or else that slowly
took the likeness
    of trees long
after the frost

and snow
have done their worst.
    The occasional ease
beneath us
    have probably
no opinions at all.
    I am not the person
to be jealous
    of such facts.
Her large eyes
    were of a blue
so pale as to
    slip from sun
to shade. Are
    you not a piper,
and far more
    aware of rumblings
around our house?
    The passengers
cross the quay
    round abandoned trucks
ejected, emptied, gazed,
    unpitied, shunned.
Whatever your opinion,
    it makes as fine
a pot edge
    as you could wish.
The unwedgeable
    and gnarled oak
tumbled out of the rapids,
    rolling over and over

on the slick rocks.
    Burly oaks projecting
from the line
    occasioned by natural
mounds or rocky knobs.
    I never did anything
of my own volition
    but forage for firewood.
I grew into want
    as careful robins
eye the delver's toil
    to see the aged
by the road-way side.
    This story will,
I fear, run
    and run.
Each did much
    such as could see
day at a little hole. Surely
    that is he
sauntering down
    to the little pier.
You must never
    go down
to the end of the town
    without consulting me.
Nothing will please
    the difficult and nice.
I must keep
    within compass
and tell him

to his teeth
I find it hard enough
   to write a mere
letter, working out
   the magnetic bearing
of each change. You
   shall find me
too far north
   for you. The fox
has run to earth,
   or, as we have it,
has holed, tunnelled
   or 'drifted'
as in one
   of the hillside mines.
It is an old story
   and a familiar,
and I need not
   go through it.
Unless 'some few'
   and 'many'
in your language
   be all one,
few philosophers
   will deny that
a degree of pleasure
   attends eating and drinking.
But I never considered
   you seriously off.

The Circle is Not Named
for Bob Hogg

The circle is not named
to be drawn in a triangle

even to the uttermost
for even the scientist

is lost in the terrible
midnight. We were

glad to get the meat
and never fashed

for kitchen. Along the
furrow here,

the harvest fell
on the table

beneath each
busy hand,

the light ceases to be
mere words

that defy the thought
of anything essential

to any of them,
sinking into

the emptiness
of mere chance.

What's the point
of reading

if it makes you feel
uncomfortable?

The table was a large
one, room yet

for a distinction
between overweariness

falling into sleep. Who's
interfering with which?

At all times an other I, that
same other. Perhaps we've

come the wrong way. The original
number disturbs

nothing
but ants about this

hill carried on
by the unseen

language is always
a mosaic work, made up

of associated fragments,
not of separate

molecules. The man
recovered of the

bite, entertained only
with the air of

words from the box
to the basket.

He had placed
a flower in a vase

on his desk. He
pretended that he

could not understand
my German. The elbow

of a hedge jutted forth, wraps
and furs lay in heaps

on the chairs,
overcoat

on the table. When
he does sit up

and takes notice
he doesn't so much

as come with a thought,
knowing that you think

it's because of my
solitary manner of life,

putting me in mind
to have these

inexpressibles altered,
who dare, like him,

to think out loud.
Those who know

how the wheels turn
are always bored

at the top
of the furnace.

Who could answer
with fewer words?

Ground to Fit
for Dorothy Trujillo Lusk

Every ship
is a romantic object,
except that we sail
in a shop which would
pack and post
your Christmas parcels.
We two have
our separate histories.
She was stopped
by a cough,
a very personal account
often embellished
by my own
imagination.

What's the matter
now the words
meshed with
each other
like oiled millstones
ground to a fine fit?
The headboard
was of monumental
walnut. Spray
with Sanfect
and you're safe.
She thus
heard at once
of Anna's exploit.

I dare say
you may be right,
so I ask you
to think
of the night
the day long.
I recognized in him
a maturity
I lacked.
She agreed
that it was
too sultry
for serious
gardening.

Dogs lost
their common
sense and barked
with a stupid
persistence,
on and on.
Fraud was
an operative instrument
in the hands
of this aspiring
general. The east
wind never fails
to disorder
my head.

Indignantly she refuted
the accusation.
We do in our consciences,
believe two and
two make four.
I didn't really
begrudge him
the food
since he was
obviously starved
of decent home cooking.
My flat is small
and also costs me
a lot of money.

I am saying,
am I not,
that I no longer
love you.
I am a stranger
in Florence,
combines
the charm
of yesteryear
with the comforts
of today
and why
could you not
run away?

In all questions
of morals,
they were allowed
to follow their
ancestral code.
The knife
or scraper
was also
made of wood.
The vine
and the wych-elm
had no pleasant
connections
for her.

I supposed
you had been out
for a healthy brisk
walk. The longest
lane will have
a turning.
Fred, she said,
it is not
as simple as that.
We get up
at some godawful
hour of the morning,
a step or two
off the hearth rug.

The gate
squeaked
at his
entrance.
The parlour
has a thick
and flowered
carpet
on the floor.
I heard
a humming
and that
a strange
one too.

No one
would be gladder
than I would
if things
ran smoothly.
Such things
tended to bore her.
I know neither
what to do
or what
not to do.
I try to do
my vacuuming
quickly.

He cited Ovid
as having said
this, and Meleager that,
in praise of a fine
head of hair.
My saying what
I'm telling you now
proves it.
According to
diplomatic sources,
they may issue
a joint statement
calling for
peace.

I returned
to search out material
for my book.
Sir Nicholas
fixed it
so we
had to turn up.
I just can't settle
to any work
as the whole thing
is a bad joke.
Let us,
at any rate,
do our part.

I was pleased
to have your letter.
My grandmother
was quiet, thoughtful,
and fond
of watching birds.
I got clumsily
to my feet, while
the whole country
fell back
into factionalism.
The midges
are at me
again.

Rocksalt Cleaves
for Louis Cabri

Rocksalt cleaves
in three
directions. I am
for you, though

it cost me
ten nights
watchings. No two
explorers agreed

about planting his
potatoes in the rain.
He re-considered
the matter,

over and over.
As daylight
began to close,
the ravens

appeared and settled
in the 'rut'
in the shade
back of the jo-house.

We were going
quite a new
road. How, then,
do we describe what

makes a metal
a metal and
a bacterium
a bacterium?

These legs have
had a day.
His long nose,
on which

the glasses
never sat
straight. In a
hole in the

ground, the chin
falls down.
The nonsense
you now

keep is enough
to turn
your hair
grey. I have

no head
for heights.
On the higher
ground there

was still little
taint in the
fresh air. He
would not have

scrupled to form
for himself
a screen out
of his own

ambiguity.
We'll game
and give
off savers

too; it's no
use getting
mithered with
waiting

on his cup.
I am growing old,
and want more
mustard to

my meat. How
did it happen
that you did not
enquire of me

myself who I
was? What's
the matter
now? The dark

areas observable
on the surface
of which none
called him to,

and none conn'd him
thanks. Eat cold
mutton, have to duck
under in any

sort of a way
must put in
a few well-placed
– ers.

If All My Woulds
for Michael Barnholden

If you can keep your head
when all persons become I.
He picked the was of shall.
Are you going to tell me
about your childhood?

Your father had an accident
there, letting the rope
feed through your hands
while yanking a borning calf
from its mother's womb.

If all my 'woulds', dear Jones,
were changed to coulds,
I have always loved drawing
goats. Edith and Olive
and me have talked it over.

What if one and one wasn't
two? A pet is always a dangerous
creature, but a sorry would,
or I knew neither what
to do, or what not to do.

Nothing dies so hard as
all the arches and whorls
and loops, all the peaks
and the troughs
and the ridges.

Please tell me a story,
just a little story,

hemmed-in between the Would
and the Should, or the Must. It wasn't
always like this? I count my
self the same man whether
I want or have. This happy

thought was considered to get
rid of blind endings. But
there are causes
and causes. I'll stick to you
like old boots

should or would.
I never would go on
a pleasure boat again
– never. The Coffee-
houses have ever since

been worn up
and worn
down. At last
the secret
is out.

No Bus in Sight
for Clint Burnham

An alarm clock
    sounds in
the apartment
    down the hall.
Outside an
    empty U-Haul,
gracelessly
    towed. If we sit
in this seat,
    it does not betray
friendship, only
    frailty. No bus
in sight. A moment,
    slightly longer
elsewhere, signifies
    now only in a
local sense. Since
    Christmas, we have
travelled one hundred
    and fifty-two million
kilometres round
    the sun, despite a
complete lack
    of upward mobility;
a penny dropping,
    exhausted by the
effort to remain
    non-judgemental,
for lack of

a better conception,
for in Wayne Manor,
    one must still
dress for dinner.
    The trains are
running late. Do
    you suppose it's
customary, no, to accumulate
    paregoric allegories
to assuage detained
    travellers? The vegetal creeper
traverses the trellis while
    we await your arrival.
What does it mean
    to understand love, for instance?
She patiently explained the
    procedure for drying
the seeds. We are at sea,
    he suggested dryly. The engine
cut halfway up the
    hill, a loose estimate
admittedly, and not
    easily conceived like
transferrable skills.
    A 20-minute ride
a year ago, but
    an old man is
still left standing
    in the light

rain. Now is the time
    to plant the bulbs, before the
first frost. What is the
    difference between
a concept and
    an idea? A reference
that only persons
    of a certain age
perceive as poetry.
    Waiting in the rain
is not poetic. She shivered
    as she sat on the
partially sheltered
    bench, a table
of schedules lay
    between them. Well,
it was him
    who clothes
the kettle, but now
    is itself cloaked. What
would it mean
    to wait demurely?
It seems that I
    have been of little
assistance in these
    matters. You didn't
notice, why would you,
    certain gestures, a preference
to make haste

dismissed out of hand, out
of time. This is what
    is remembered when we
listen to music. Was that
    you? There were noises
they didn't particularly
    want to hear getting
through the thin
    walls, everyone living
in the building
    at once. At one
time the bus went
    directly downtown, but
there are silences throughout
    the night, a subtext
circumcising our living
    situation. She gradually
sifted through the newspaper
    notices, acclimatizing to
the cold rain. Put
    the wood in th' hole
from a sub-dialect indifferent
    to the hours of listening
to another's television, a
    din not yet remote,
or a responsive relief,
    not the repeated thud
of parietal lobe
    rubbing against the idioms

of a certain school
        conflicting with the
familiarity of neighbours.
        A loin-cloth left behind
in the bus shelter, drops
        of rain making riverlets
on the windows
        of the train, obscuring
the view, but loving it
        just the same. Anticipating
a particular gesture, parsed
        peculiarly. At what
point do we admit
        we're mistaken? I thought
I saw the orange lights
        of the bus, but perhaps
plastic caps cast
        reflected light, wooden
slats surrounding the
        concrete slab on which
the structure rested, for
        in that instance I was
convinced he was a changed
        man. His grandmother
would exclaim 'for the love
        of God' while his father
would mutter 'crissake,'
        an epithet for any
eventuality, absent

a viable alternative,
members only.
       What if I said
I like peeling
       potatoes? The placement
of your hands
       suggest you may be
uncomfortable
       with this suggestion.
Was it gorily
       depicted or were
sensitivities misplaced?
       She was wearing
a military surplus
       jacket when we
met. My corner
       of the desk
was overrun
       with stacks, so
I had to balance
       it on my thigh.
He spent hours in
       silence attempting
to master the daily
       puzzle, but I was more
surprised than puzzled,
       thinking we could catch
the last bus, but
       of course the lateness of

the hour had eluded
     him. Don't we always
have a situation?
     Considering the predicament
in which she
     found herself, the notion
of melting into a crowd,
     the crow's evening migration,
without a pot to cook
     it in, and the dinner
was only a small failure.
     Of greater significance
was the complete lack
     of envy for the kettle.
This was a conversation
     he wished to avoid, for
he found it impossible
     to explain his lethargy.
If the current is cut,
     there will be no
bread, the bills remain
     unpaid. No allowance
for allergies, the joy of
     others through these
flimsy walls has no
     paregal, what?

A Lute and a Lyre
for Nicole Markotić

Would you know the difference
between a lute and a lyre?

Did he radiate the terror
that prevarication brings

when replying to such questions?
Yet the quality suggested by

a pneumatic drill does not quite
accord with the liar's paradox.

Were you, perhaps, a ringside
paramour? All her

autobiographies suggest
a casual lust, although

vapid desire might also be
suitable in these occasions.

What tends to be spoken in such
moments automatically

defers to idiomatic
equivocation. If you

prefer a jump-start, I would
suggest the quail skewers.

My insides are out of order.
My outsides depict a man

comfortably in his 50s,
although the dinner jacket shows

signs of wear. Perhaps we should
signal for car service. From

the far side of the lot, it
was difficult to get a

visceral sense of what went
awry. Still, we squinted and

wondered at the long ricercar
that shocked and left each of us

somewhat aghast. An astute
listener could discern the treat

of a clandestine fugue, but
if it were me, you wouldn't

have recognized the frugal
treatment afforded to this line

of questioning. A quiet
adagio can carry

far, but formal attire yields
despairing discomfort. We

all want to cry but wont of tears
is teased from the unsuspecting

attendant who smirks while
suggesting a coat check. For

if we admit ghosts, then
this hotel is teeming. And if

the planets align, do they form
a quixotic team coming

together to be set in
popular songs? If I doubles

for us and you doubles for
them, then who doubles for those

who didn't buy the book? Now
that is something to sneeze at.

We may have to double back,
finding reason, but no rhyme.

And yet he rhymed off his reasons
with such detachment, the echo

subsided almost as quickly
as I read the onscreen news

screamed as though doubt was left to me.
We decided not to attend

the performance which was
nevertheless unavoidable.

We deemed the matter closed, or
perhaps I am mistaken.

I'll have to get back to you, but
did you mean me when you said them?

Was it the knees that tease
from the far periphery,

and your rhizomes that tasted
of tar? Do you remember

just how far we have gone? And
so we strained for a hint of

a motive or a suggestion
of harmony before the horns

came walking back into the picture,
but there can be no coda.

He liked a twist or at least
an unmet expectation.

A motet to arouse an
emotional shrug of the

shoulders, a crossing of the
arms, or even a craning

of the neck. What is left when
the music ends? A small sedge

of cranes by the shore, seeming
to exhibit complete

disinterest. Is it such
a problem to believe, when

watching the sunset, that the sun
will appear in the sky again

tomorrow? Do you prefer
a king's pawn in online play?

The delaying move failed yet we all
witnessed the hesitation,

more becoming much less. An
analogy to armies

will only, my friend, stymie
appreciation, more struggle

than dialogue, a responsive
algorithm. For weeks we

awaited Fred's reply, the
ritenuto fell into place,

but such a tremendous fall-
ing. The alteration between

tension and release witlessly
breathed yet shunned. He suggested

tweaking the lease, but the ricercar
returned. They seemed a bit fried,

yet flexible, lax even.
Our seats were in the wings

and with a wonderful air of
ease one leaned into the sense of

staggeringly sustained sounds;
we now were fewer than when

we began the film, the questions
no longer lengthened the lines

that sent us to seek in other
works a particularly

permeable yet arresting
eek.

Parsnips
for Catriona Strang

drawing to a traffic circle,
the peripheries, tallying turnabouts
going by, I thought we said you
but misheard nowhere

perhaps they should ride –
on what side, in which gear
we said excepting those already
sided in particular

when listening is needed
the bike picks its own rider,
but a fickle seat can rile
and expose the gulf between

passengers and riders,
yet cantilever or won't may not
be the setting one wants
when the sighting of a bus

in the distance doorings
are on the increase while
disc brakes render no ideas,
but indecision bolsters a sense

of the steady effort of the hill
to the easy pull of the slope
but no one spoke of the
slipped gear unconvinced

it is a good gauge of utilitarian
empathy; still one could eagerly
navigate an empty path on an
unpadded seat; what say you

to a continuous trek where
every stop eventually unceases
or until a final rest to assess
is there no one we do not love?

Ought

for Ted Byrne

No ought from
a gee whizz,
not from an
if only either.

With only a
scant familiarity,
his parents
settled

on Ulysses.
The sycamore's
obligation, if you
will, differs from

the owl's, yet
neither it nor
the sparrow
sees the similarities.

As a child, he
would seize any
opportunity to
slip the knot

leaving none the
wiser, but
got on without
a dropped word.

From a bird's
eye view such
machinations are
achingly acute,

if the owl's grief
is measured
against the
griffon's.

From early on, we
grasped a rough
intuition, a raft
of rules not quite

a code. A coddled
owlet – this hope
becoming a nested
expectation.

An old woman
reading Beckett
on the bus.
What was

I supposed to do?
Waiting for neither,
by god, it was
difficult to live up

to his name, dispossessed
as he was of courage,
cleverness, and conceit.
Consequently, the heart

of the problem
was not easily
pierced, grasping only
a blunted understanding.

I kept my knives
in the knife-box, gently
rubbed my hands
and whispered something —

something about flesh
and wine, but my
companion began
to sing. One does

not need to be
a saint to break
bread with the poor.
A poor comparison

made poorer still
by the single-minded
conceit; a sympathetic
glance is no

substitute for a
continuing contract.
We were barely
noticed when we

slipped in late,
with time to fulfill
our familial functions,
a confessional

monologue missed
all my marks. We
left over-nourished
but under no

illusions that an
enlarged heart is
the same as a
generous one.

At this stage
any strange
deposition is
unwelcome. No

edicts either to
deter fate. The rough
ground is not
to be smoothed

bit by unbidden
bit. He answered
the call, or rather,
there was an

answer to a
call, side-stepping
the scorpion's
sting.

Well then, what
account can you
give? To chase
the response,

you must return
the call. His parents
were forgiving of
all but him, or

so it seemed. Did
you turn down
the offer? For what
it's worth, the antidote

is not always laughter,
while the anecdote
you are seeking,
even after we've

forgotten the imagined
freedom to take the
time to carefully
consider Kantian imperatives

from the swallow's
perspective, pondering
the malady most
likely to curb this behaviour.

The road might not,
in fact, be as hopeless
as it seems; nonetheless
a habit is not necessarily

an addiction to its
demands. As the sparrow
flies so the cure for
prescription. Sometimes

the journey is immaterial
when being there is what
matters most. If there is
no ought out of is

from this,
what if
a simple delight
in the dilemma?

Many, Not Any
for Robin Barrow

My title is deliberately
    equivocal. Assuming that I
have got the broad
    facts right, this story
is revealing. This is not
    a facetious point, because
actually I see myself
    as a (utilitarian) liberal,
communitarian in
    the process of coming
to the sad
    conclusion that
there is no entirely
    satisfactory solution
to what I shall call
    the problem
of cultural domination
    either in principle or,
a fortiori, in practice.
    Reference to
'design', rather than,
    say, 'planning',
already hints
    at the sort
of precision
    and inflexibility
that is required
    when producing
specifications for

an aeroplane, rather
than the openness
        and unavoidable
equivocation
        to be found
in the stage directions
        for a play. Some
of what I say, I
        confess, does strike me
as fairly obvious
        and incontestable.
'Everything
        is predetermined'
would be an example
        of the former;
'There is life
        on another
planet,' an example
        of the latter.
If this is broadly
        convincing, it follows
that the mere
        creation
of democratic
        structures
is of no necessary
        importance.
Let us start,
        unashamedly,

with basics. This
        desire for
publicity
        perhaps, in part,
explains a new
        emphasis on
the so-called
        'public intellectual'.
The view that
        an educated
person should have,
        in Juvenal's words,
'mens sana
        in corpore
sano' dies
        hard. It will be
seen that this
        is not a new
battle. Rectitude,
        not to say
self-righteousness,
        there is in plenty,
with everything
        from drinking
to abortion. Such
        a view is now
widely scorned.
        No doubt
a question

     that for many
of us
     it would be nice
to be able to
     answer. I find
this premise
     truly extraordinary.
These objections
     differ in kind
and plausibility.
     Yet, unusually
in such a case,
     I cannot
say that I
     feel that overall
it is a particularly
     illuminating
or useful
     volume. In other
words, it
     is not simply
a matter
     of taste
or subjective
     opinion that Sibelius
is an important
     composer, da Vinci
a genius, Donald
     Bradman a great

cricketer, or Brunel
     a leading
engineer. Who else
     these days
appreciates
     that one should write
'sorts of reason'
     rather than
'sort of reasons'
     or
'sorts of reasons'?
     Professor Scheffler
is altogether
     too sanguine
and accommodating
     to metaphor, slogan,
and analogy.
     There is no ghost
in the machine.
     Am I not
constrained by
     reality?
What, for example,
     constitutes stealing?
I do not,
     incidentally,
think that
     'practical
judgement' is
     in any way
a less

obscure term.
Personally
    I don't particularly
mind the smell
    of it,
nonetheless, I
    recognize
that the smell
    of yesterday's garlic
is offensive
    in a way that
the smell of roses
    is not. I cannot
rid my mind
    of the image
of a frustrated
    dog pursuing
a somewhat
    unimportant flea.
I do not see
    that William James
and his squirrel
    have got
much to do
    with the issue.

For, if in fact
      the bridge won't stay
up, the cake won't
      rise, or the child won't
learn, then something
      must have been wrong
with the theory
      that said that
it would.
      There are
times when one
      feels that he
really believes that
      if only chaps
would pull their socks
      up and do some
simple conceptual
      work, we could
avoid the horrors
      of a Rwandan
or Kosovan
      conflict.
There is no
      conspiracy theory
here. They have
      no tablets
to bring down
      from the mountain.

More and More
for Isaac

how does one
account for the blue
isaacs among
the jacqueminot
a minute aftershock

the hedge-sparrow
was crestfallen
yet not one of them
will fall to the ground
and scarcely kept

from tears
an undeserved curse
goes nowhere
not pinnock not goldfinch
not rook nor crow

even the hairs
of your head
the haunts of certain hay-
zick are all accounted
and cast out

like an unfledged
dunnock deflated
the general mood
with memories
of her migration

as a sparrow
as at sunrise
in its flitting
finds a home
and the welfare of certain

pearly eggs
and callow fledglings
whose father I remember
shone exhilaratingly
restored

a sense of gentility
anxiously urged
to bustle along
but lay among
milkweed

what can he mean
by the lambent
pupilability
and the nest
and the proceedings

of some ground-bees
astounded as we were
by a sky the colour
of a hedge-sparrow's
egg

as though unperturbed
by the slow, low, dry chat
and maybe a person doesn't
no...maybe not

Sometimes Welcome

such as
we aim
we aim
a clouded grasp
or an else
a shameful else
or else reasons
sometimes trouble
anything senseless
we aim
we aim without
anything less
perhaps less
lest we grasp
nothing else
if just
nothing

proven
for meaning
rejection amends
though hastily unwritten
sometimes I think
if meaning
lacks belief
or disobeys
or forgiveness

intentless
yet why not
disagree not
as rules grace
but as warning
any warning
graces
any grace
sought
entreated

others understand
error sometimes
after each confused
each shuddered intent
oversteps nothing
borrows inarticulate
afterthought
the unwritten trust
others crave

who nowhere
or near
and indeed unwritten
or aware
will aim
at least
clutching
upon each
each end
ends each
further
or

clearly futile
without some
dependent warning
depends upon
constantly inarticulate
constantly failing
such disobeyance
sometimes
awareness graces
least if unwelcome
what yielding
what most
thwarted

not such
unwritten urge
just senseless
wounded risk
else yearn
each mended guess
aims to prove
my urge
just thwarted
carelessness
disagreed
nor misguided
your public
risk risks
this misguided
mind

without
until without
failed thoughts
sometimes
welcome belief
until failed
failed until
sensed
sometimes
sometimes
from belief

haltingly
equal as
none equals
none nothing
yearns but
sometimes
we madden
each shameful
question so clearly
wrestled
a dubious we
equal to those
unfailingly
inarticulate
unfailingly
constant

These Constant Moments

the senseless wound of unfailing conviction
bears nothing until reason is risked

confused and shamefully misguided
we grievously disobey

we taught clouded urges but knowing
we shared a terrible gasp

believing we lacked such awareness
sometimes troublesome

our mended neglect
neither worse nor disagreed

rejecting the reasons
you lack

what is sometimes unwritten
contriving a last guess

not misguided aims
or inconstant forgiveness

from futile confusion
an unfailing oath

you disagree terribly
till questionless trust

sought grace
not as nowhere

a bitter intent overstepping
a rigid warning

clearly these unwritten rules
sometimes shudder

craving after
an adequate will

nothing trusts
a borrowed grace

these inarticulate thoughts
others have fallen against

give neither belief nor
a clouded carelessness

the mind's forgiveness
furthers abhorrence

alone or not
this careless wound

sometimes
is sensed

as if ritual annoyance
was understood

I at least
yield

to inarticulate
belief

if you depend
on these

unwelcome convictions
these constant

moments
some borrow

a public grief
proves futile

an unwritten warning
a just question

not confused
not alone

if nobody denies
each obtuse other

Elegy I

And yet and if
as with few

and frolic
courteous riddles

nor pampered play
but if

inhabits
another house

Elegy II

love all things
though small

and were these
one

that in one
must as

yet
an anagram

can never be unfit
nor justly absent

like clouds
like none

Elegy III

although good
works

have sealed
nothing

should undo
that apostasy

confirm yet
forced open

unprized
if unknown

as foxes
and goats

change when
they please

more hot
wily wild

bound idly
apter to endure

their own
and yet allows

love
but forces

opinion
nor every

one run
a wild roguery

Elegy IV

Once and but once
all supposed escapes

questioned
all catechized

through with glazed eyes
as though hope

were seen
close and secret

still to sleep
and watch

and return
and would seem kind

and search
and find

and fearing
to name strange notes

sighs and sweats
confess

yet remove
and skipped

and ingled
in oaths

and only then
never witness

or
forbear

    even my shoes
    were speechless

Elegy V

take my thoughts
though you

like me
but when

we both
when my hand

and my head
with care

within
and scattered

may seem
judging

and delicate
in which

by whom
seem

Elegy VI

serve so
still

enriched
and where

none sways
such names

not by oaths
breathed

curled carpools'
embrace

and beckon
such scarce

visiting
entirely doubtful

or speechless
swell

to gape
in gallant scorn

in flattering eddies
in that resolute state

Elegy VII

subtle
difference

of sighs
sounds cast

or changing
devisefully

speechless
mutely and mutually

remember
an hour's discourse

could scarce
answer and

torn sentences
chafe for others

Elegy VIII

as in a still
chafed

as the balm
such sweat drops

and sets
all the rest

lying or
warts or wheals

round on every
rough-hewn

first within
slender stands

quivering
or rough-barked

quarters like
lamentable acquisitions

equal in the
comparison

Elegy IX

tolerable else
transitory sought

any lank sack
whose shade

whose holes
whose several places

hate extremes
yet I would

rather wear out
my hill

than ebb
without end

Elegy X

image of more than
makes and makes

impart the more
the less and gone

conveniently
fantastically

which locks up
and locks out

nothing
with none

Elegy XI

not for
nor for

nor that
links knit

nor but
the bitter

which admit
nor yet

strayed or
gone to gain

to comfort
circumcised sentences

negligently left
or lets

or avails
a slyly

subtle
or slightly

sombre
or entirely

uncertain
some scheme

in tenements
content with

changed
necessities

for form
gives none

and their form
is gone

on
alone

Elegy XII

all I owe
chance if

the least
comfort

have I
company

overcome
ransom or rather

reasons why
some wither

and some
sake nothing

still we
redeem or

rather
promise more

like lambs
a fresh wit

or spent sighs
a blissed breath

brings down
the rain

all my groves
groans

or shades
in one

another
their own

again naked
compassion

seen clear
as snow

Elegy XIII

obscureness
to boot

each form
or some

such some
mutual sifting

to impute
or rather

sooner now
seen

or watched
streamed

amiss maybe
where one sad

truth sighed
so ambushed

over all
our becks

winks, looks
our feet

often far
from our

words in
riveting

vulgarity
never strain

nor suggest
much more

but not
many

Elegy XIV

kettled envy
yet in

vain evens
out

an escape
or inveighs

how to listen
mildly lived

to limn
with a pen

for nothing
spills

which includes
countless cavils

or inevitable
errors

Elegy XV

I sing
no harm

reformed or reduced
juggler or justice

no grease
nor will be any

too many
fitting for the feat

apprehending tends
to kind

acquaintance
to sort discourse

fit for so fine a
plaguey custom

trafficked apace
urged to speak

set in
one met thought

present
to any

praise
but put to push

for pay
trades hope

when privileged
protections

make the rest all poor
yet proves

none could
stay

to take
nothing but

refused
and made away

though willing
found weary

standing still
to dwell

barely promised
the very sign

Elegy XVI

doubt
breathed

because
the matter

but made
in water

and both
have thought

so many
formed into words

so many
among

so many
sealed

and empty
forfeit

to break
or quit

the wrong way
except

circumstances
might cease

teeming
and forget

an urge will
bin streams

before you
alter yours

but drift
each simple word

and wander
until uttered

all flung
a longer pleasure

not in made work
nor while

those times
never lengthen

with intent
all of which

were such subtle
pastimes

softly
by chance

Elegy XVII

strangely
ensued

our long
starving hopes

persuasive
remorse

calmly begged
impetuous

page
and kind

leave
left behind

roughly read
and shivered

unurged
nothing

nor change
nor mind

discovering
quickly indifferent

to walk
in expectation

except to
think it

    enough

Elegy XVIII

in motion
why should

I so much
with many

diversified
sitting

in light
sheds

what else
ever so

contented
in change

clearer
where their

fair-spreading
strangely

pursues itself
all alone

love
the liberal part

but follows
a hard choice

the last
holds

such agreements
have

another's worst
obtained

though ends
the attempt as

accounted charity
to stir up

indifferently
unkempt kindred

not exempted from
our weak credulity

formless at first
but fashions

spoiled
yet frequently

only some few
retain the seeds

of modern censures
for service

amongst the least
declined

whatever form
the message came

nor change
weighing some

left ever
alone

Elegy XIX

whoever
we err

like perfection
prefer first one

and then
to think

they're not
but if

we stray
every sphere

is not there
and contemplate

centrically
or worthy

or more fit
as infinite

as fetters
becalms us again

where we
wrinkled our

rosy hemisphere
swelling to

where they seem
cleaving between

two successive
clamouring

to descry
some scattered

sailing in
that stay

though the current
should set

no further
consider this

misspent symmetry
lovely enough

to stop
but not stay

and change
never change

the first part
transplanted

as far as
the air resists

so aversely laid
to which

this empty
and ethereal

error gives
sway

Elegy XX

come come
defy until

I labour
ofttimes tired

with standing
off glittering

but a far fairer
world spangled

which you wear
for that harmonious

envy can still
stand

such uncertainty
softly in this

used walk
we easily know

before behind
between above below

these bonds
are due to

unbodied bodies
cast in

court that
like pictures

or coverings
we imputed

this ruinous
line knowing

there is no
penance

   due

A Gloved Moment

contradict the connection indifferent coercion
uprooted relentless objection awakening to the
insufficiencies grasping the merely speculative
a rented diction as false as any line

its pristine emphasis as familiar as any endeavour
deviant or indecisive circulates each sentence
each stumped ceremony displaced or implied
it is only as it is

the discomfort of the dissonance twists or scaffolds
failure or fissure harsh and unfamiliar hollowing nor
embedded chit-chat magnificent and classed from
itself a setting out already departed

arbitrary impediments gloved to my hand rubbed
merely resembles but proceeding rather a ramp
already worth stuttered inversion clusters and gloves
groping in anticipation

producing the play of the p's the hand that hastens
interminable partition presupposed trajectory
but unceasingly suppressed an interrogated impasse
insofar as what was no longer is

repeatedly cached this detail divided yet garnered
by fingers gloved with tottering testimony removed
from traffic a finite moment culpable of yet more
chatter that the mere nothing is not

murmuring dispersion of matter yields its tendency
surges up collapses between the more and the less
fervent repetition against repressive constraints
unfolded no longer knowing what to recognize

breaches ruin all determinations enjoined induced in
silence the mark then tendency of suppression nor as
satisfaction between the moment as thought assumes
the same stroke infinitely limited

internal division within which contradiction thrilling
as song circular if merely to mention elevated relief
eminently mistaken in making or in a casual instance
when each belief breaks with what it believes

instead or finding apparent yet parsed suspends even
moiled guttural dealt cleaved coated or taut edged
active a necessary undecidable of all cavalier without
accent the question can be conceded

deferred and diverted the truly feigned in fewer
between fetter with indispensable anticipation
interiorized in terse yet torqued such unsuccessful
shots within which everything is stitched

or sensible hearth feigned rigorous or scours
then renders near cost not layered at least remains
restricted particulars of all pure pressures these acts
for which we've already acquired a taste

and scaffolded what activates this belief too fleeting
to become detached or danced stands out finally
almost ungraspable remains fettered then understands
form is form

nor retained subject and predicate parcelled out
brands preens weaves with tangled tracings coiled
round in reverse between chainings seem improvised
this too weakly disguised content

in an instant by contingency our insisted memory
more ample than handled the necessary sifting this
strict incidence implied or entirely incessant may
strike certain ears with suggestive sonority

escaped every necessity nor between arbitrary and
motivated all assurances taken out of the frame forced
surge and sense cleaves consequence always subtle or
naïve sumping the remains of a detached collar

seems ceaseless that push between tendencies content
to converge alleged a soiled predicate cuts the
quick-step a movement hands the hemmed glove a
question of sumptuous practice speaking for itself

closing conceived as complete or claiming to circulate
a mistake imagined standing for sound
this assimilation of expressions tilts elevated variance
as certain as such things are

inferred from showing doesn't suffice
nor dismisses a practical doubt not dealing but
delegated though acquainted with contributions
resting on forced assumptions

any mistaken giving grounds that sound quite slight
straight off a breath topples all trace fused into
follows this shunned judgement an informed murmur
the old misunderstanding

swallowed circumstances as intrinsically obvious
stands fast or liable to shift a shared reliance but
determined movement mutual as implied procedure
proved to pay for this wayward bewitching

but tempted to reduce no longer assures neither
sheath nor scratch absents nor alleges nor delegates
but tightens the benefits of a bit of force imagining
so much being

closes the sluice or outflows the very instant forces
grafts an infinitive scene without ridge or scar
a sign of fatigue no longer scaffolds
a gloved moment conformed

Five Minutes Ago

corrected consequences rubbed harmonic
elevations hamper monied variance chanced
impede belief til my hand in your glove

    thus we expunge
    the sentences that don't
    get us any further

necessary pretense that distorted notion that
ethic without work distorted nine to five desire
a different self surmised authority torqued to sire

    yet we encounter
    such unsuccessful shots
    at every turn

fervent contradiction a slight breath straight off
shunned uncertain traces topple all judgement
fused into the foundation surpassing aporia or

    doubt
    gradually loses
    its sense

oppositional apprehension feigned an
instantaneous dissociation a hole in my thinking
this essential excess only as it persists

fluid propositions harden
and hard ones
become fluid

supposed instinct a counter turn a slogan
supported across insofar as it has been
shunted onto unused consent or deceit

    the river-bed
    of thoughts
    may shift

interminable resistance or remainder
porous, permeable, and indeterminable
partition this door no longer home

    doubting
    presupposes
    certainty

petitioned impasse stepped up or
through not edged not nervous
without trajectory

    much seems to be
    fixed and removed
    from traffic

staged support circulates this
strange possessive a gloved hand
or mine this paged portion

    how little
    of yourself
    is left to you

awake and watching immensely
demarcated for tedious doubt
expunged further before

    a mistake
    becomes
    something forbidden

thinking totters the subordination
of questions terse testimony
inclined to complicate or believe

    all sorts of slogans
    will be used
    to support our proceedings

or suspend a certain viability a
tenuous grasp spent and curtailed
accordingly or merely surmised

I mean these words
as I did
five minutes ago

Notes and Acknowledgements

I would like to thank the editors of *Open Letter*, *West Coast Line*, *Ottawater*, *Touch the Donkey*, *Periodicities*, and above/ground press for publishing earlier versions of these poems.

I would especially like to thank Louis Cabri for his advice and patience in preparing these poems. I also want to thank Geoffrey Gatza for his assistance in preparing the manuscript for publication and James Sherry for his support. Additionally, the support and encouragement over the years of Robyn Laba, Isaac Manery, Michael Barnholden, Clint Burnham, and rob mclennan has been invaluable and appreciated immensely.

The source for the vocabulary in "Equivocation" was the Jesuit *Treatise of Equivocation* written by Father Henry Garnet in 1598. Garnet was executed in 1606 for his role in the Gunpowder Plot. The manuscript I used was prepared by David Jardine in 1851. A chance operation was used to generate an initial text that was then heavily edited.

Gilbert Ryle's *Dilemmas* was the source text for the vocabulary used in "Dilemmas." A chance operation was similarly used.

"Let's Sit Down and Lie to One Another" is a collage of exemplar sentences found in the *Oxford English Dictionary* that use variants or synonyms of the word *equivocate*.

"As They Say," "The Circle is Not Named," "Ground to Fit," "Rocksalt Cleaves," and "If All My Woulds" are part of a series of embedded poems. These poems are a kind of cento in which passages are taken from other sources to create the text. Each of these borrowed passages contains a word from a poem by the dedicatee, so that each word in the dedicatee's poem appears in the same order in the created text as they do in the original poem, although the words are often rather far apart.

"As They Say" embeds a portion of Peter Culley's "Winterreise" from *The Climax Forest*.

"The Circle is Not Named" embeds Bob Hogg's "Three Rooms" from *Heat Lightning*.

"Ground to Fit" embeds Dorothy Trujillo Lusk's "Let My Voice Thud Throughout the Land" in *Ogress Oblige*.

"Rocksalt Cleaves" embeds Louis Cabri's "Clone Jacking" from *The Mood Embosser*.

"If All My Woulds" embeds a section from Michael Barnholden's *On the Ropes*.

With "No Bus in Sight," "A Lute and a Lyre," "Parsnips," and "Ought," I discontinued the use of source texts, except for the poems by the dedicatees that are embedded in the texts.

"No Bus in Sight" embeds a portion of Clint Burnham's *Pandemonium*.

"A Lute and a Lyre" embeds Nicole Markotić's "langsam" from *Bent at the Spine*.

"Parsnips" embeds Catriona Strang's "7 clubs" from *Reveries of a Solitary Biker*.

"Ought" embeds the first section of Ted Byrne's "The Rilke Versions" in *Duets*.

"Many, Not Any" consists of passages taken from published articles by Dr. Robin Barrow. The poem was composed with deep appreciation for the clarity and rigour of the philosophical analysis, as well as the humour, and indeed, the poetry of Dr. Barrow's writings. This work is also written with immeasurable gratitude for the friendship he has shown me over the years.

The source text for the vocabulary in "Sometimes Welcome" and "These Constant Moments" is Sophocles' *Antigone*, translated by Elizabeth Wyckoff and edited by David Grene and Richmond Lattimore. Again, chance operations were used.

The Elegy poems draw almost all of their vocabulary from John Donne's Elegies (Signet Classic, edited by Marius Bewley). Each elegy in the series corresponds to the same numbered elegy penned by Donne.

The indented lines in "Five Minutes Ago" are taken from Wittgenstein's *On Certainty* (Harper Torchbooks, edited by G.E.M. Anscombe and G.H. von Wright).

Robert Manery lives in Vancouver, BC on the unceded and unsurrendered territory of the xʷməθkwəy̓əm (Musqueam), Skwxwú7mesh (Squamish), and the Səl̓ílwətaʔ/Selilwitulh (Tsleil-Waututh) Nations, where he is the editor of *Some*, a print-only poetry magazine. He is the author of *It's Not As If It Hasn't Been Said Before* (Tsunami Editions), and the chapbooks *Richter-Rauzer Variations* (above/ground press), *Many, Not Any* (Some Books), and *Elegies* (above/ground press).

Made in the USA
Columbia, SC
28 January 2024

30361645R00090